BRENTA

and Veneto Villas

arsenale editrice

Editorial co-ordination
Arsenale Editore

Photography
Mark E. Smith
Archivio Arsenale

English translation
Peter Eustace

Brenta
and Veneto Villas

First Edition January 2009

© ARSENALE EDITRICE

Arsenale Editore Srl
Via Ca' Nova Zampieri, 29
37057 - San Giovanni Lupatoto (Verona)
Italy

Introduction

Early in the XV century, the Venetian Republic began its process of expansion into the mainland of the Veneto area, which saw the Serene Republic extend its territories in the hinterland even as far as Bergamo and Crema. The new geographical discoveries also coincided with a general change in the international political scenario, characterised by the expansion of the Turks.

It was in this context that the "Veneto Villa" came to the fore. Changes in trading routes, political necessities, the availability of new lands and the steep rise in agricultural prices throughout the 1500s: all these factors gradually prompted Venetian nobles to turn their attention from the sea, that sea which for centuries had been the main source of power for the Lagoon people. Inasmuch, the expansion of the "Veneto Villa" is the architectural expression of this turning away from the sea. Venetian aristocrats, not the least influenced by the feudal mentality of the mainland nobles themselves, began to build residences that combined two functions: a source of agricultural income and a refuge from frenetic city life (even in those times!), a niche for platonic "otium" and healthier living.

Many 1400s villas were based on Venetian models but were soon followed by the villa-temple – conceived by Andrea Palladio – and the villa-palace.

1600-1700s villas continued these consolidated designs and gave special emphasis to the central main hall.

The monumental villa as the evolution of the villa-palace was characteristic of the 1700s and also coincided with the final period of the Republic, while neo-classic Palladian architecture marked the end of this parabola.

Via Catajo, 1
Battaglia Terme
☎ 049 9100411

1. Casa d'Este, also known as «Castello del Catajo»

The Catajo complex takes its name from its location on the Sieva hill by the River Brenta at the feet of Euganean hills and originated from a villa with a loggia overlooking the canal where Beatrice Pia degli Obizzi held an elected and cultured literary salon. Her son Pio Enea I, was a general of the Serene Republic and fell in love with the view from this standpoint. He added a tower-belvedere higher up, with halls decorated with frescoes by Giovan Battista Zelotti depicting the war-like deeds of Pio Enea and his ancestors. These works were directed by Andrea Della Valle from 1570 to about 1573. Its external appearance resembles a fortress, with turrets, merlons/crenellations, triumphal arches and a drawbridge.

The imposing building at the back, thus creating two levels, required demanding levelling and terracing work. A large park between hills and valleys, crossed by the Rialto stream, was used as hunting reserve. Marquis Pio Enea II also held the property in high regard, to the extent that after he inherited it in 1648 he worked for eighteen years to extend and renovate it. In 1803, the last of the Obizzi, Tommaso, who has also embellished it - among other things with collections of weapons,

Casa d'Este

coins, paintings, musical instruments and archaeological finds - bequeathed it to the Duke of Modena. In the hands of the Hapsburgs, who also extended the building (but transferred the collections to Vienna) so that the Villa ultimately boasted 350 rooms on four floors.

The land included theatrical fountains of the 1600s and late 1500s, such as the splendid fountain of the Elephant, statues, masks, aviaries, a maze of hedges, a loggia with seventeen arches facing the canal, hanging gardens, loggias, terraces, a fish pond, a swimming pool and the large Giants courtyard below ground level once used for naval performances, tournaments and spectacles. The exterior frescoes have been lost.

2. Villa Garzoni, Michiel, Carraretto

*Via Liston, 6
Candiana,
Pontecasale
☎ 049 5349602*

Around the mid-1400s, the Venetian Garzoni family purchased land south of Padua and for about a century dedicated themselves to expanding the property and reclaiming the swampy areas until Alvise Garzoni decided to build his noble residence. It was probably built between 1537 and 1550 to a design by Jacopo Tatti known as Sansovino (1486-1570). The architect, Florentine by birth and Roman by experience, arrived in Venice after the Sack of Rome in 1527 and introduced a breeze of Classicism in the city: the style was already well-established in the city of the Popes. Sansovino was responsible for the true "modernisation" of the appearance of St. Mark's Square, representing the power of the Serene Republic, with the Library, the Mint and the Loggetta. This is the only example in which he was involved in a villa.

The prospect of the villa has elements in common with the two-dimensional style of Venetian palaces, as if the sides were not intended to be seen and with the aperture of the central sector between two lateral blocks. Behind the facade, through the arches, there is a progressive breach where the arches are repeated in depth to create a telescopic prospect terminating in the countryside. The central sector therefore does not match the typical Venetian passing salon but an interior courtyard in the Roman style. The facade comprises a base wainscot for protection against floods, arrangements for service facilities and two noble floors, with three series of ribbed windows in the lateral parts and a double central portico with five arches set off by a trabeated order of semi-columns, Doric at the bottom and Ionic at the top. A broad staircase followed by arches lead to a loggia, which repeats the same arcade before closing beneath a portico, that in turn repeats the same arches before leading to the square courtyard, flanked by two other identical perpendicular porticos and a wall opened by windows around a huge garden, with the same five axes reiterated from the facade. This is the loggia of the facade, therefore, that is multiplied, in parallel or at right angles, to create the entire volume of the building. In the final analysis, this building is dominated by the taste of *invention* and surprise by then essential in Roman architecture: an enormous palace on the outside, the interior resembles a concert of open and semi-open spaces that sacrifice the closed settings, relegating them to a relatively narrow section of the wings, a device well-suited to a summer residence.

Villa Garzoni,
Michiel, Carraretto

3. Villa Barbarigo, Pizzoni Ardemani

Via Diana
Galzignano Terme,
Valsanzibio
☎ 049 9130042

This complex stands in the small basin of Sant'Eusebio in the eastern Euganean hills and is surrounded by a lush amphitheatre of hills; it boasts, as well as the most famous and documented Veneto garden of the 1600s, the largest and best preserved tree maze in Europe.

Work to arrange the garden, measuring 1,500 sq.m., was begun by the Contarini but the current appearance was developed about 1669 by the Barbarigo brothers: Antonio, senator and procurator of St. Mark, and the blessed Gregory, Bishop of Padua.

The area is divided into quadrants by a longitudinal axis of about 400 metres which, passing through the Villa, continues to the top of the hill with an avenue of cypress trees, intersected at about two thirds by another path marking the lowest point of the land, where three fish ponds slope down, and with other perpendicular axes. Kiosks, belvederes, exedras, aviaries, hornbeams, maples, ilex, oaks, elms and cypresses grouped or in rows along the avenues and paths create walks, small clearings and peaceful meanders. The statuary indicates a delightful and educational itinerary: the island of rabbits, the fountain of the swan – symbols of fertility and purity –, the

*Villa Barbarigo,
Pizzoni Ardemani*

hillock of Time, the small, octagonal fountain in red marble with numerous statues, the square with plays of water.

The fulcrum of allusions and allegories, the maze or labyrinth of dense boxwood hedges is square, measuring about 3,000 sq.m., with a route of 1,500 metres, concentric in parallel lines, that must all be walked to reach the centre (like earthly life towards good and its painful trials). The Bath of Diana is very interesting and embellished with statues; it was originally the water inlet at the end of the crossways axis. The Villa is rather small compared to the rest of the complex and follows the more traditional outline of such 1600s-1700s buildings in the Veneto.

4. Villa Cortuso, Maldura, Emo Capodilista

Via Montecchia, 16
Monselice
☎ 0429 781987

The Villa was built in 1588 and is traditionally attributed to Vincenzo Scamozzi. It comprises a very simple, isolated block, a raised floor reached by two ramps of side staircases linked on ground level with a tetrastyle pronaos with an indented tympanum, coat of arms and columns with Corinthian capitals in terracotta. Originally, this was the main prospect facing the Battaglia canal, with access from the water to which it was connected, and the Villa stood clearly on the embankments; the latter were later substantially raised and the situation, as for many complexes standing on the banks of waterways, is now inverted – the embankments are now higher than the building. The garden was re-arranged and the two original fishponds have been restored.

5. Villa Giovanelli

Via Cappello, 241
Noventa Padovana
☎ 049 625066

The Villa, built in the late 1600s perhaps by Antonio Gaspari, presents an upper floor and two mezzanines with four simple axes per side, while the three central sides are protected by a colossal, hexastyle Corinthian pronaos on columns, surmounted by a tympanum with a coat of arms

Villa Cortuso, Maldura, Emo Capodilista

and statues on the acroters, a semi-octagonal base to which Giorgio Massari in 1738 added a majestic staircase and six statues on the balustrades by Antonio Tarsia, Antonio Gai and Marino Groppelli.

The double height salon has frescoes by Giuseppe Angeli, now in very poor condition, stuccos framing paintings and medallions in the lateral rooms. The garden also dates from 1738, once famous but now very depleted, embellished by a gate, labyrinth and pavilions.

6. Villa Molin, Capodilista, Conti, Dondi dell'Orologio, Kofler

Vincenzo Scamozzi began building this villa in 1597 for the Venetian ambassador Nicolò Molin, on the bank of the Battaglia canal near the Cagna bridge. The building is central with a square ground plan, with another square hall in the middle, the side of which has a 1:2 ratio with that of the external perimeter and develops in height through the coverage to emerge with a body having a square base and a spa on each side to illu-

Via Ponte della Cagna, 106
☎ *049 8670344*

minate the salon. The prospect towards the canal is, however, substantially emphasised by the presence of a significantly protruding Ionic pronaos, without direct access from the ground, with a coat of arms in the indented tympanum, the horizontal cornice of which continues the line of guttering, and statues on the acroters. This imposing volume shifts the centre of gravity of the building and interferes with its centrality, thereby orienting it significantly towards the water. The other prospects, in short, are very different and the sides are only highlighted by simple serlians. The gently bossed wainscot was sacrificed as the land was raised – a frequent event in complexes close to waterways.

The hall is completely decorated with frescoes. Scamozzi's garden still survives with 1700s statues and fountain, the park and court.

During the First World War, the Villa was home to Military High Command and it was here that the armistice document was prepared and then signed 3 November 1918 in Villa Giusti.

7. Villa Contarini, Camerini

Via Luigi Camerini, 1
Piazzolla sul Brenta
☎ *049 5590347*

This is one of the most majestic buildings in the region, presumably involving a Palladian project of 1546 for Francesco and Paolo Contarini for the central block. As of 1676, Marco Contarini – a procurator of St. Mark – radically modified the complex, with the decoration of the central body, the addition of lateral wings and outhouses, the transformation of the east wing into a gallery with telamons on a rustic order, covered by a terrace embellished with statues; other statues are found in the park, on the balustrade of the fish pond and the aedicules of the nymphaeum with alternating arched and triangular tympanums, some enclosing niches, others with gratings towards the wood.

The Villa was not only designed a "place of delights", of humanist *otii* in contrast to *negotii*:

the stream animating the garden irrigated the rice fields and drove the mills, the mangles of the blacksmiths and the silk mill. In 1680, Marco Contarini conceived the large hemicycle square opposite the villa, with a portico on heavy rustic columns, for the fairs, which was half-finished at the end of the century. There were also two theatres and a concert hall with a particular acoustic system that made it possible to hide the musicians.

The garden in front of the facade was redesigned with large parterres and a central fountain in 1868 by Eugenio Maestri for Luigi Camerini and the one at the rear by Lupati and Oblach in 1892 for Paolo Camerini, who until 1924 turned Piazzola into a model town with important industrial factories and homes for workers between gardens and vegetable plots. There is still the lake with the island and its mound with a bronze of Christ by Luigi Bistolfi. The current appearance retains the heavy Baroque of the Contarini lightened by the Liberty and eclecticism of the Camerini.

8. Villa Cornaro or Corner

Via Roma, 35
Piombino Dese
☎ *049 9365017*

Andrea Palladio designed this villa in the 1550s for Venetian aristocrat Giorgio Cornaro, yet developments also continued beyond the end of the century. The model very closely resembles Palladio's only other work in the period – Villa Pisani in Montagnana – although here he enjoyed all the necessary conditions for freer development. The double order of loggias, Corinthian on Ionic, becomes wider to become hexastyle and protrudes from the wings, themselves also symmetrically elongated from the central block; the loggia is repeated again in the inside at the rear and correspond to the central hall, again with four columns and sculptures by Camillo Mariani (1593-1595) in the niches, here not vaulted but with beam ceilings. It is introduced by 104 frescoes by Mattia Bortoloni (1717) for Andrea Cornaro and stuccos by Bortolo Cabianca; a fine garden with flower beds, fish ponds, porticos and loggia, as well as rural facilities.

9. Villa Duodo, Balbi, Valier

The last stretch of Via del Santuario climbs the hill to Rocca di Monselice, passes through an arched gate – the Porta Romana – and then enters the Duodo estates. Pietro Duodo, the envoy of

*Villa Contarini,
Camerini*

Venice to the Holy See, obtained permission in 1592 to demolish a convent of nuns to which the area belonged and build with his friend Vincenzo Scamozzi the Villa and new church of San Giorgio completed in 1605. The church is also the last station of the Cross in a "Holy Way" of six small chapels, later known as the seven basilicas of Rome (excluding St. Peter's); a pilgrimage to the place – thanks to a privilege granted by Pope Paul V in 1605 – ensured the same indulgencies obtainable through the visit to the basilicas in Rome itself. The small square in front of Scamozzi's Villa and church around 1740 saw a new wing built by Andrea Tirali (1657-1737), the architect of the churches of San Nicola da Tolentino and San Vidal in Venice. He added statues and reliefs to embellish the original serlians of the villa's facade, giving rise to excessive theatricality caused by the difficulties of inserting such rather bombastic elements into a substantially plain framework. Towards the Rocca, or fortress, a majestic exedra with an imposing staircase embraces the square of the villa, with a central fountain. The square is home to the busts of three Duodo family members, set in niches and the work of Alessandro Vittoria.

*Via Sette Chiese
Monselice
☎ 0429 72468*

Villa Duodo, Balbi, Valier

10. Villa Emo Capodilista

The Villa can be defined as truly unique since the building has a perfectly symmetrical central ground plan.

For centuries, the high plateau of Montecchia and the surrounding land had been owned by the Capodilista family and in 1568 Gabriele commissioned the building of painter and architect Dario Varotari (1534-1596), of German origin and a disciple of Paolo Veronese, who at the time was working on a cycle of frescoes in nearby Praglia Abbey. Varotari levelled off the top of the hill to create an Italian garden with square, quadri-lobate walls on the side axes that materialise and cross in the centre: they start off as staircases from the perimeter, continue as avenues, enter the square ground plan villa, cross a loggia and return to form staircases, that in the heart of the building – the centre of the ground plan thus divided into four identical quadrants and at half height – pause on a landing and turn at right angles along the perpendicular axis to reach the loggias on the upper floor on the other two prospects of the building. The result is a square ground plan with four double loggias with five arches, between Doric strips on the bossed ground floor, four pseudo-turrets at the corners

Via Montecchia, 16 Selvazzano ☎ 049 637294

Brenta and Veneto Villas

and crossing staircases in the centre defining four square room on both floors; on the perfectly identical prospects, the appearance of the turrets is veiled and refined by streamlined scrolls coupling with decorative elements, with an Oriental and fairy-tale effect. Together with Antonio Vassillacchi known as Aliense (1556-1692), Varotari also painted the frescoes in the interiors; the Villa room depicts the other properties of the family; elegant motifs in the Rocaille style were added in the 1700s. Nearby, there is still a Mediaeval castle with an imposing tower rising in the centre and a small 1500s church; the court is home to a museum of rural civilisation. Tradition suggests that was home to the difficult meeting between St. Anthony and Ezzelino da Romano in the presence of the blessed Giordano Forzatè, an ancestor of the Capodilista. These Paduan nobles joined the aristocratic Venetian Degli Emo family to found the Emo Capodilista branch.

11. Villa Olcese, also known as "Dei Vescovi"

The Villa was apparently commissioned by Venetian Bishop Francesco Pisani, through the humanist Alvise Cornaro – who between 1529 and 1538 was his administrator – of Giovanni Maria Falconetto (1468-1534), who had already worked successfully in Padua for Cornaro. First built in these years, it was probably completed around 1542 by Andrea Della Valle, who designed the outhouses and the compound wall with monumental gates with upside-down arches and stone spheres as in Badoera and Villa Garzoni. The Villa stands in a panoramic position amidst the Euganean Hills on a relief once home to a Mediaeval castle, whose foundations were exploited. The slopes were also exploited to create staircases and terraces that form an interesting complex with the outhouses. The noble body is an imposing block with a square ground plan with two floors, refined by apertures that ensure full en-

*Via dei Vescovi,
Luvigliano
Torreglia
☎ 049 5211118*

Villa Olcese, also know as "dei Vescovi"

joyment of the landscape. The ground floor has false bosses in brick, with arches on pillars and staircases with several ramps that form complex architectural motifs on the two main and opposite prospects; this floor rather resembles a high basement that supports a single, true and clearly distinguished storey. The upper floor is structured like a loggia with five arches on straight bases squared off by Doric strips, with twinned strips at the corners, on these prospects, with entirely frescoed interiors, in part saved thanks to restoration work, attributed to Lambert Sustris from Amsterdam. The flanks repeat this motif but without the open loggias, replaced by windows centred inside arches. The distribution does not have bilateral symmetry and the passing Venetian salon was retained, with heads in the two loggias, together forming a double T, doubling the Venetian palace model that always had a single main prospect and lateral halls.

12. Villa Tiepolo, Passi

Via Brigata Marche, 24 - Carbonera
☎ *0422 397920*

This complex, built for Almorò Tiepolo – a senator and procurator of St. Mark – is made up of the villa with symmetrical lateral adjuncts turning at right angles, linked to the main body by double loggias with three axes; they form a broad courtyard with flower beds and a central fountain, set in a park with a "tempietto", stables, greenhouses, fountains, small lake, busts, ornamental vases and statues attributed to Giuseppe Bernardi known as Il Torretti (1694-1774), the *maestro* of Antonio Canova.

The Villa is an early-1600s block perfectly similar to a Venetian palace: it has central mullions with balustrade and two single windows per side with small balusters; there are central doors – above and below – with arches, with adjacent jambed windows having rectangular inserts above to form a decidedly Venetian style that recalls the overlapping of two serlians. The ground floor has rectangular windows and the main floor ribbed windows – and up to here all levels correspond to those of the adjuncts which, however, have only jambed windows. The Villa also has a third floor added or in any case in part raised at the end of the 1700s, with the same rectangular windows as the ground floor and the same small balusters of the second floor, terminating in a dormer with a ribbed single window, strips, a small surmounting fronton and linking Baroque scrolls. The loggias linking with the wings were also probably added in the late-1700s. The triple mullion on the main floor corresponds to the central salon, as always in Venetian palaces; this hall is decorated with 1700s frescoes having mythological subjects between painted prospects and stuccos also of the 1700s; there is also XVII and XVIII century furniture and furnishings.

13. Villa Tamagnino, Negri, Lattes

The Villa – built in 1715 for Count Paolo Tamagnino – was one of the first works of Giorgio Massari; it was later home to architect himself and was then inherited by the Negri Counts, who sold it in the mid-1800s to the Lattes family. Massari (1687-1766) was a Venetian and is considered to represent the transition between the

Via Nazario Sauro, 50
Casoni,
Istrana
☎ *0422 738159*

Villa Tiepolo, Passi

Palladian tradition, which he reviewed through the work of Baldassare Longhena, and neo-Classicism. The noble home with two storeys rises to a third storey, with a serlian protruding into the crowning tympanum (only in the median part) linked to the second floor by two arc-like wings reaching the edges of the building terminating in stone spheres on plinths. The entire central sector seems to be integrally extrapolated from the facade of a typical Venetian palace, with serlians surmounted square inserts. At the sides, two symmetrical outhouses with arches on exedra pillars join the surrounding wall to embrace the oval Italian garden with statues, basins and a chapel on the south-west side, with altarpiece and ceiling by Amigoni, a high relief with the portrait of Tamagnino and two paintings by the Piazzetta school. The outhouses are linked to the central body by an arcade per side, surmounted by a terrace marked off by a baluster with putti at the corners, and contain two metal coats of arms of the Doges of the Dolfin family, a fountain with two columns and putti topped by another coat of arms in marble with the seal granted by Napoleon to one of the Lattes family, the grandfather of the last owner, who bequeathed the

Villa to Treviso City Council. The wall has fragments of marble and terracotta from the excavation works for Rio Novo in Venice. The Villa is richly furnished and still boasts collections of art, especially oriental, with rare items, a picture gallery, ancient clocks, an extravagant collection of musical boxes and mechanical toys, musical instruments and a portrait – probably the only one – of Giorgio Massari.

14. Villa Barbaro, Basadonna, Manin, Giacomelli, Volpi

Strada comunale Bassanese Maser
☎ *0423 923004*

The Maser territories came into the possession of the Barbaro family in 1339; the Villa was commissioned of Andrea Palladio around 1560 by brothers Daniele and Marcantonio. This complex stands out significantly from Palladian villa production: it does not stand in a central, flat position in the middle of the estates but towards the margins on a slight slope; it does not reflect the hierarchical outline of buildings determined by functions, so that the noble quarters continue into the outhouses, normally used exclusively for rural purposes, and the lateral dovecotes masked by the facades with sun dials crowned by a tympanum and lateral connections with upside-down arches compete with the body of the main, central and protruding body, without a pronaos with free columns but over two, not significantly emphasised levels, framed by a tetrastyle Ionic order with semi-columns and tympanum of exaggerated proportions, with a central balcony protruding into the trabeation decorated by a high relief in stucco with the family coat of arms.

It seems that all this can be attributed to the desire of the patrons to recreate a classic villa, based on Pliny's descriptions of his Villa Laurentina and modern interpretations of Roman antiquities in the 1500s. An element that distinctly recalls the Eternal City is the nymphaeum: at the rear,

there is a small, rectangular secret garden with a semi-elliptical basin in the centre, leading to a circular grotto with the statue of a river god. The other, distinctly "Roman" element is the "tempietto", on the road to the south-east, dated 1580 with a circular ground plan: a Pantheon in miniature, with the same cubic proportion and similar elements, the pronaos, the stepped dome, apses alternating with aedicules inside, with statues in stucco by Vittoria e two outside in "tenera" stone by Orazio Marinali.

The exceptional character of the complex also arises from the pictorial cycle on the main floor by Paolo Veronese, helped by his brother Benedetto and workshop assistants.

15. Villa Giustinian, Ciani Bassetti

Via Roma, 131/133
Roncade
☎ *0422 708736*

The Villa was commissioned by procurator Girolamo Giustinian of the Santa Barbara branch about 1489, after marriage with Anesina Badoer, whose family had owned buildings and land in the area since the 1400s; it is likely, however, that work was not completed until around 1520, because of the war against the Cambrai League fought bitterly on "firm land". The new complex

may possibly be attributed to sculptor-architect Tullio Lombardo. Earlier Mediaeval structures are recalled by towers at the corners of the massive masonry walls with Ghibelline merlons and a moat and cylindrical turrets at the entrance that give the overall site a rather unusual appearance. The body of the villa reflects the Venetian typology, with a basement, two storeys with ribbed windows with simple, flat cornices and a mezzanine with square windows, facade with nine axes divided into three sectors, of which the central one stands out for the lightness of the double, protruding loggia, with three arcades on columns, crown vault underneath and caisson ceiling above set off by the tympanum. The western and southern prospects have external frescoes damaged by bombing during the last war and restored in 1947 by Mario Botter.

The interior has many rooms with beams and banded frescoes. The Oratory of Sant'Anna (1542-1543) attributed to Santo Lombardo, son of Tullio, has busts in terracotta of the founders, Girolamo and Agnesina, commissioned by their son Marcantonio Giustinian and likely the work of Jacopo Sansovino. The large courtyard in front

Villa Giustinian,
Ciani Bassetti

of the Villa is currently arranged with two English lawns at the sides of the avenue leading from the entrance bridge to the portico, flanked by 1700s statues, and two, small Italian gardens flanking the stepped loggia; this courtyard is marked off by the wall where the entrance is inserted by two large, symmetrical outhouses against the perimeter, with an arched portico, and in front of the villa by edges continuing the line of two frescoed walls that closed the secret side gardens as far as the small, square "brolo" or orchard-vegetable garden; everything was surrounded by the larger "brolo" or rural compound.

16. Villa Emo

The Emo family boasts ancient origins and arrived in Venice as early as 997, from Greece; the "Serrata del Maggior Consiglio" in 1297 acknowledged the noble status of the family; in every period of the Republic, the family provided eminent figures who occupied the highest positions of responsibility in the government. This family has always owned this villa and has always lived here. Leonardo Emo, chandler for Terraferma (as the Venetian hinterland was called), lieutenant of the Veneto army and governor of Friuli in Udine, in 1535 purchased from Andrea Barbarigo an estate of about forty hectares that he irrigated by exploiting the water of a canal from the Brentella to convert crop-growing from sorghum to maize. Leonardo decided to erect a suitable, noble and agricultural building on the estate for himself, the country people, livestock and harvests. Inasmuch, its architecture is not that of the *otii* of the nobility. Yet Leonardo did not have the chance to bring his innovative ideas to fruition, since he died in 1539 – it was his grandson Leonardo, first-born of also deceased son Alvise, who in 1556 and only about 20 years old, built the home to designs by Andrea Palladio.

Villa Emo and Villa Barbaro at Maser are the only

Via Stazione, 5
Fanzolo di Vedelago
☎ *0423 476334*

Brenta and Treviso Villas

Palladian examples having the straight layout of residential and rustic buildings, with a central, noble body, always without a protruding pronaos but here with an internal Tuscan tetrastyle loggia, with the family coat of arms in stucco by Alessandro Vittoria in the tympanum that in this case only surmounts the portico. The noble floor was completely frescoed by Giambattista Zelotti – a student of Paolo Veronese – probably between 1561 and 1565. The furnishing is original 1600s-1700s.

17. Villa Manin

Piazza Manin, 10
Codroipo,
Passariano
☎ 0432 904117

The second half of the 1700s saw the construction of the last yet grandest villas in the Veneto as the swan-song of Venetian domination over the hinterland. 1800s production rather focused on country houses having a more apparent than formal bond with the century-old villa tradition, especially the mansions of the "firm-land" bourgeoisie. Villa Manin symbolises the fall of the Republic in two ways: its owner:, the last doge Lodovico Manin, announced the end of the Serene Republic of Venice on 12 May 1797; and it was in this villa, chosen as his general headquarters, that on 17 October Napoleon signed the Treaty of Campoformio. The majestic complex was begun at the end of 1600s and only completed around the mid-1700s. The entrance, to the south, crosses a bridge over a large fish pond, flanked by two towers at the heads of two wings of outhouses with porticos, with arches on pillars and trabeated strips forming an exedra embracing a large lawn; two constructions at the end of a crossways axis create a spatial pause like theatrical backdrops, then another compound closes the main courtyard, with two other wings of outhouses facing each other, through to the final screen, perpendicular to them, of the imposing body of the villa.
The park continues at the rear towards the north,

Brenta and Veneto Villas

again marked off by two towers, with greenhouses, fish ponds, orange and lemon groves, a garden, century-old plants, small lakes and hillocks; and everywhere, even on the architectural elements, in the chapel and the sacristy, sculptures by Giuseppe Toretti and his assistants Francesco Bonazza and Pietro Baratta. The villa has stuccos, tempera and frescoes by Louis Dorigny and other artists.

18. Villa Foscari, also known as "La Malcontenta"

This is the most typical example of the villa-temple, the only Palladian one on the banks of the Brenta and entirely in the province of Venice. Built for Nicolò and Alvise Foscari around 1560, after various episodes even culminating in a state of total deterioration, it is now owned again by the descendants of the same family.

It stands in isolation in a large park, with a cubic form and north-facing main prospect, close to the right bank of the Brenta, raised on a high wainscot (a Palladian expedient to protect noble quarters against floods) and dominated by an hexastlye, Ionic pronaos with two other lateral axes; the innermost one is reached by climbing two symmetrical and right-angled staircases. The tip of the fronton reaches the guttering line of the building, surmounted by a further attic-dormer with three windows and tiny strips and a second tympanum – an absolutely anomalous element for Palladio but common in the Treviso area.

The southern facade facing the garden mirrors the northern one but its central part, corresponding to the pronaos, is barely emphasised with an indented tympanum interrupted by a large 'termale', that with three doors underneath suggests the design of a large, single arch; the lateral windows and the dormer are repeated. The interior is dominated by a cross-like salon extending from the internal facade of the pronaos to the facade at the rear, while at the sides it is de-

Via dei Turisti, 11
Malcontenta,
Mira
☎ 041 5470012

Villa Foscari,
also know as
"La Malcontenta"

limited by six, symmetrical rooms of decreasing dimensions. The noble floor was entirely frescoed by Giambattista Zelotti and Battista Franco: these frescoes have suffered greatly over the centuries and even recent restoration work has not managed to regain their original, integral appearance. During the 1600s-1700s, the Villa was extended by creating a kind of square enclosed by a portico on three sides; the demolition work by Austrian troops occupying the Villa in 1848 returned the complex to its initial status.

19. Villa Soranzo, also known as "La Soranza"

Via Naviglio, 5
Fiesso d'Artico,
Barbariga

Standing on the left bank of the Brenta and despite its name, the Villa was only owned by the Soranzo di Rio Marin family between 1611 and 1671. An undocumented tradition attributes the frescoes of the facade to Benedetto Caliari (1538-1598), brother of Paolo, despite the evidently later style overly rich in majestic illusionary effects and agitated figures, and the stuccos and fireplaces in the interior to Alessandro Vittoria. The internal structure and distribution, with the passing T salon and side rooms, like the apertures in the facade, grouped in a serlian at the centre and tightly locked between ground and first floors, and lastly the external fresco decorations perfectly match the model of the Venetian palace, in particular between the 1500s and the early 1600s; the staircase and dormer with double Baroque scrolls are later additions; there is no longer any trace of the annexes.

20. Barchesse di Villa Valmarana

Mira Porte, Mira
☎ *041 4266387*

The 1700s property of the Valmarana, on the right bank of the Brenta opposite Villa Seriman, focused on a cube-like, three-storey building without any type of decoration, with two symmetrical and aligned outhouses, a central body with Ionic strips terminating in a flat trabeation and lateral porticos with pillars and paired Tuscan co-

lumns. In the late 1800s, the Villa was demolished to avoid payment of a tax on luxury homes, while the outhouses/guest facilities were left to ruin. The one on the right, located in a meander of the Brenta and thus with two prospects over the canal, was recently restored and contains a large hall with late-1700s frescoes with architectural scenes, allegories and landscapes, once attributed to Giandomenico Tiepolo but now to Michelangelo Schiavone from Chioggia known as Chiozzotto.

21. Villa Farsetti, Selvatico

Via Roma, 1
Santa Maria di Sala
☎ 041 487550

Villa Farsetti resembles a French rococo castle, with the typical physiognomy of the late "international" baroque; it has three storeys, with Doric parastades and a terminal balustrade on marble modillions, developed symmetrically in line from the central, ellipse-like and double-height salon, that protrudes into the facade with a convex surface, with Corinthian columns and parastades and an orchestra gallery. Two wings with two concave floors are linked by monumental porticos with 38 columns in Greek marble probably from the Temple of the goddess Concordia in Rome. At the rear, the rustic order outhouse and guest facilities are intentionally disguised. The garden was very impressive, with colourful flower beds, citrus fruit bowers, numerous statues, a lake with a tiny island, a hippodrome, theatres, amphitheatres, bridges, streams, fish ponds, rare grape varieties imported with their own soil, highly-prized crops, copses, a place for naval battles, a turret, aviaries, Roman spas and much more.

Filippo Farsetti (1703-1774), whose by then Venetian family actually had Tuscan origins, embraced an ecclesiastic career to avoid the political career expected of his rank so that he could dedicated himself to the study of arts and sciences and to collecting; he travelled widely and collected numerous chalk models of antique sculptures

Villa Farsetti, Selvatico

which were even studied by Antonio Canova; in 1733, he inherited the Sala estate which he suitably extended and irrigated so that, after obtaining from the Pope the precious columns mentioned above, he turned to Paolo Posi, the Roman architect and stage designer actually born in Siena. These works were carried out between 1758 and 1762, alongside those on the botanical gardens and their wealth of greenhouses with citrus fruit and very rare exotic plants, including "magnolia grandiflora" today so widespread. A part of the building is now home to the offices of Santa Maria di Sala Local Council and the Civic Library.

22. Villa Pisani, also known as "La Barbariga"

In 1620 and later in 1661, the Pisani dal Banco Venetian nobles declared among their properties a country estate with annexes and land in the village known since the previous century as Barbariga, on the right bank of the Brenta; the earliest available image is a print by Vincenzo Coronelli (about 1709) depicting what is now the central part of the Villa – a classic Venetian building comprising a ground floor with seven axes, a mezzanine with five, a dormer with ribbed window and balustrade, a fronton with acroter vases and lateral pinnacles, and simple, flat cornices of doors and windows; a rustic annex, an orchard/vegetable garden and an Italian garden facing the Brenta.

The engraving by Gian Francesco Costa (1750) al-

Via Barbariga, 45
San Pietro di Strà,
Strà

ready illustrates modifications and extensions: terraces on the wings, the rustic annex turned into living quarters and a re-modernised garden; works continued and documents dated 1772 also mention painter Jacopo Guarana. The original core is decorated by delicate, multi-colour stuccos, fireplaces with figurative tiles, frescoes, ceramics, mirrors, delicate chinaware and grotesques in the French rococo taste. The elegance of the interiors was never hinted at by the rather plain and identical prospects.

Lastly, two long wings were built that also include large halls for feasts; the facade over the Brenta only has a median fronton on its characteristic side. The facade overlooking the garden is more imaginative, with plays of strips and paired, trabeated Ionic columns, small triangular frontons intersecting with rectangular apertures and alternating with elliptical slots, steps and balconies, with two tympanums reflecting those on the opposite facade with acroter vases.

Work is also documented in following years, when the family engaged architect Giannantonio Selva for the chapel and perhaps also the re-arrangement of the garden and the English-style park; the Clock Tower in axis with the Villa on the other side of the path at the rear is by Giuseppe Jappelli.

23. Villa Foscarini, Negrelli, Rossi

The Villa was built by the Foscarini noble Venetian family after 1617 and prior to 1635, at point along the Brenta opposite the bridge leading to San Pietro di Stra, flanked to the west by a tributary of the river. The building is rather broad and the facade is divided into three sections: the two lateral sections have a double central axis and one simple axis, with two obelisks per side on the roof over the solid walls; the middle section is three axes wide and preceded by a protruding pronaos, with a high, delicately false-bossed wainscot cladding the entire ground floor, with an upper tetrastyle Ionic

Via Doge Pisani, 1-2
Stra
☎ *049 9800335*

Brenta and Veneto Villas

Villa Foscarini, Negrelli, Rossi

pronaos three axes deep, surmounted by an indented tympanum with a flat cornice in line with the frame and acroter statues. The pronaos once had two ramps of staircases descending to a floor raised on a mezzanine; the bossed storey continues into two symmetrical wings with large arches crowned by a balustraded terrace. These wings, the conversion of the most mezzanine level into a single ground floor, new fresco cycles and other renovations and restorations were commissioned by the aristocratic Negrelli family of Verona, who were the owners in XIX century. The central section corresponds to the passing salon in the Venetian style. The prospect over the garden reflects the one over the Brenta but is not bossed, has no central protrusion and Ionic semi-columns that are also repeated on the ground floor.

The guest facilities in the garden, with arches set off by Tuscan strips and perhaps originally outhouses, had two apartments and an imposing hall for festivals (lacking in the villa itself) with impressive frescoes by Brescian perspective artist Domenico Bruni (1591-1666), while the figurative cycle is attributed to Pietro Liberi. At the end of the garden there are the stables, perhaps commissioned by Marco Foscarini (Doge 1762-1763) and possibly designed by Giorgio Massari (1687-1766).

24. Villa Pisani, also known as "Nazionale"

Via Doge Alvise Pisani, 7 - Stra
☎ *049 502074*

The Pisani di Santo Stefano family had owned several properties in a bend of the Brenta on the left bank since the early 1600s, where a small villa was later built. In 1719, a project by Girolamo Frigimelica Roberti (1653-1732) was probably ready for a colossal villa for brothers Alvise and Almorò Pisani that involved the demolition of the existing building in 1720; yet it seems that is was only in 1735, when Alvise was elected doge, that a mew project was commissioned of Francesco Maria Preti (1701-1774) and in the same year building work started that only came to an end in 1756. At the end of the garden, connected at the rear of the Villa by a double, tree-lined avenue also used as a hippodrome but later replaced by the present-day water basin, there are the stables, another work by Frigimelica probably completed between 1719 and 1721. The Villa and its 114 rooms is not only one of the most grand and elaborate villas in the Veneto but also one of the most atypical: it does not have the traditional

*Villa Pisani
also known as
"Nazionale"*

character of the Venetian home and the ground plan with five wings and two interior gardens is an evident development of the concept of the Baroque regal palace. The facade is very clearly articulated: the central ledge with colossal Corinthian semi-columns, tympanum, frieze and festoons, contains the double-height ballroom; two symmetrical wings with four axes of windows and paired strips terminate with two protruding bodies with four strips and tympanum that are also the heads of the perpendicular wings. The ground floor is more or less bare and the decorations begin with the staircase and its Greek divinities in wood.

The ten-hectare park designed by Frigimelica is still extant and is a superb example of 1700s gardens in the Veneto, with a geometrical layout rich in focal points and perspectives. Yet the masterpiece of the Villa is the ceiling fresco of the Apotheosis of the Pisani family, with the Parrot and pairs of male and female satyrs in the ballroom commissioned in 1760 of Giambattista Tiepolo.

*Via Palladio, 1
Lonedo, Lugo di
Vicenza
☎ 0445 860613*

25. Villa Piovene, Porto, Godi

The attribution of this villa is the subject of considerable controversy. Some claim it is Palladian, since it is so close to the first villa he designed, others mention Godi, Porto, Piovene, Valmarana and Malinverni; the Ionic hexastyle pronaos dates back to 1587 and the wings are characterised by extreme simplicity. The setting is extremely delightful and enhanced by the theatrical yet very gentle staircase leading from the rich lower gate to the majestic, tong-stepped pronaos. They were all, like the side outhouses with streamlined Doric porticos, designed around 1740 by Francesco Muttoni, while the numerous statues are by Orazio Marinali. Tommaso Piovene was the first principal, while Count Antonio Piovene, an architect and owner in the 1800s, refurbished the romantic park. The Oratory of San Girolamo dates back to 1496.

26. Villa Barbarigo, Loredan, Rezzonico (Town Hall)

While the design of the villa, built between 1588 and 1590, is attributed to names such as Palladio and Scamozzi, the unknown architect was probably not from Vicenza but Venetian. The building is

Villa Barbarigo, Loredan, Rezzonico (Town Hall)

imposing and can be considered as an arbitrary Baroque interpretation of the formal Palladian heritage: how can we not think, in the complex play of Tuscan and Ionic colonnades and the paired columns – that in any case continue into the outhouses surrounding the "square" – of Palazzo Chiericati in Vicenza. The triple ledge of the central section hides a cubic nucleus, cut horizontally by the sequence of Tuscan colonnades and vertical streamlined by the staircase, the overlapping of the loggias and the extravagant detail of the exaggerated and "almost" angular cusps. The interiors have frescoes by Antonio Vassillacchi and Antonio Foler.

Piazza IV Novembre
Noventa Vicentina
☎ *0444 788520*

27. Villa Almerico, Capra, Valmarana, also known as "La Rotonda"

Although completed by Vincenzo Scamozzi around 1585, it is among the villas that best keep faith in terms of construction with the original project by Palladio, probably dated 1566, and the most representative Palladian villa long since a model – even though it was commissioned by High Prelate Paolo Almerico as a city palace and published as such by the architect in his treatise. The Villa summarises several of the special features of Renaissance art: first and foremost, the practical resolution of the ideal type of building with a central ground plan – which had involved leading architects in the 1400s-1500s – accentuated by the roundness of the central hall and the hinge of the dome, that actually in the designs of *The Four Books of Architecture* by Palladio were higher, thereby better responding to the centripetal function, balanced by the centrifugal function of the four Ionic pronaos. This centrality was suggested to Palladio by the location of the Villa, dominating a spread of sweet, crop-growing hills, thereby ensuring the effective and delightful principle of harmonious insertion in the landscape. Yet the building is another synthesis theorised and sought after during the Re-

Via della Rotonda, 47
☎ *0444 321793*

naissance and later – the synthesis between the arts: architecture, sculpture, painting and landscaping are all effectively embraced: the external statues by Lorenzo Rubini and Giambattista Albanese, the fireplaces decorated by Bartolomeo Ridolfi, the frescoes by Alessandro and Giambattista Maganza, Ludovico Dorigny and Aviani, stuccos by Rubini, Ruggero Bascapè and Domenico Fontana and the separate chapel attributed to Carlo Borella are all inserted in a garden landscaped in the English style.

28. Villa Bertolo, Valmarana, known as "ai Nani"

This complex actually comprises three buildings. In 1669, jurist and literary figure Gian Maria Bertolo commissioned a small building, by Antonio Muttoni from Lugano, that enclosed the north courtyard: a rather plain, central staircase reaches a terrace surrounding the noble floor to form a kind of wainscot around the building, five sets of windows grouped yet well-spaced in the centre, with a single mullion window per side, with a short crowning tympanum and statues on the acroters, that is repeated on the rear prospect. In 1720, the property came into the

Via dei Nani, 8
☎ *0444 321803*

possession of the Valmarana Counts, who commissioned a "foresteria" or guest facilities in the centre, with seven arches on bossed pillars linked by a broad atrium with a colonnade of Tuscan columns, and imposing stables with a triple nave to the south, probably by Francesco Muttoni, Antonio's son. The name of the Villa derives from the eighteen statues of dwarfs by Giovanni Battista Bendazzoli, dated about 1765, aligned on the surrounding wall, that in turn has rustic bossed bands. Yet the reputation of the Villa especially derives from its pictorial cycles, completed in 1757 by Giambattista Tiepolo in the halls of the original small building and by his son Giandomenico in the "foresteria", with the collaboration of Gerolamo Mengozzi, known as Colonna. The two Tiepolos in these frescoes each had the chance to express individual inspiration and demonstrate their distinctive characters: Giambattista populated the small building with Olympian heroes and divinities, while the art of Giandomenico is expressed in domestic and country-life scenes, balls, gypsies, charlatans, Chinese items and exotic figures in picturesque and Rococo landscapes.

Villa Fulcis, Montalban

*Via Safforze,
Cusighe, Safforze*

Villa Buzzati, Traverso

*Via Visome, 18
☎ 0437 926414*

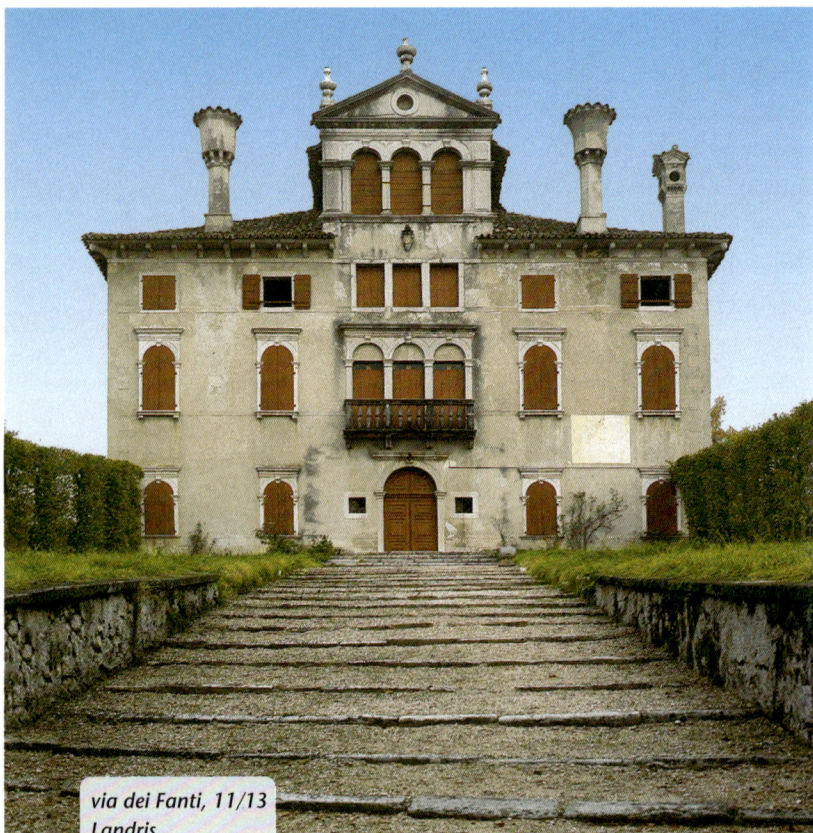

*via dei Fanti, 11/13
Landris
Sedico*

Villa Rudio, Milanesi

Villa Widmann

Piazza Marconi, 63
Bagnoli
☎ 049 5380008

Villa Selvatico, Emo Capodilista

Via dei Colli,
Sant'Elena
Battaglia Terme
☎ 049 8721650

Villa Roberti, Frigimelica, Bozzolato

Via Roma, 102 - Brugine
☎ 049 5806048

Villa Pisani, Placco

Via Borgo Eniano, 1
Montagnana,
Borgo San Zeno

Villa Badoer, also known as "La Badoera"

Via Giovanni Tasso, 1
Fratta Polesine ☎ 0425 668523

Villa Molin, Bragadin, Grimani, Guerrini, Avezzù

Via Zabarella, 1
Fratta Polesine
☎ 0425 668030

Via Alessandro Selmi, 543
Polesella
☎ 0425 444968

Villa Morosini, Mantovani

Villa Di Rovero

Via Bordignon, 8
San Zenone degli Ezzelini

Villa Giustinian, Salice

Via Giustiniani, 11
Portobuffolè

Villa Zeno, also known as "Il Donegal"

Via Donegal, 11
Cessalto, Donegal

Villa Ferretti, Angeli, Nani Mocenigo

Via Brenta Bassa, 39 - Dolo
☎ *041 2501495*

Villa Rocca, Ciceri, Bressan (Hotel Villa Ducale)

Riviera Martiri della Libertà, 75
C. Musatti, Dolo
☎ *041 5608020*

Villa Torre-Donati, Recanati, Olivieri, Zucconi, Fracasso

Via Naviglio, 25
Fiesso d'Artico, Barbariga

Villa Seriman, Foscari Widmann-Rezzonico

Via Nazionale, 420 - Mira
☎ *041 5298711*

Villa Cappello, Giantin

Via Doge Alvise Pisani, 6
Stra, Fossolovara

Villa Della Torre, Cazzola

*Via della Torre, 19
Fumane, Verona
☎ 045 7701461*

Villa Allegri, Arvedi

*località Cuzzano
Grezzana, Verona
☎ 045 907045*

*Via Santa Sofia, 1
Pedemonte, Santa Sofia,
San Pietro in Cariano, Verona
☎ 045 8001835*

Villa Serego, Alighieri

Villa Saraceno, Caldogno, Saccardo, Peruzzi, Schio, Lombardi

Via Final, 8 - Agugliaro
☎ *0444 891371*

Villa Rezzonico

Via Cà Rezzonico, 66
Bassano
☎ *328 5864307*

Villa Chiericati, Da Porto, Ongarano, Rigo

Via Nazionale, 1
Grumolo delle Abbadesse,
Vancimuglio

Villa Pisani, De Lazara Pisani, Ferri

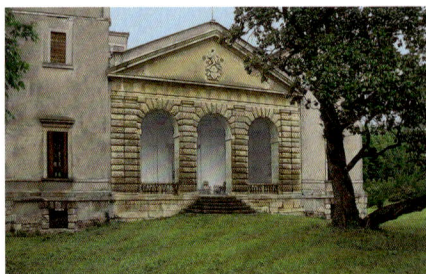

Via Risaie, 1
Bagnolo di Lonigo
☎ *0444 831104*

Villa Godi, Porto, Piovene, Valmarana, Malinverni

Via Andrea Palladio
Lugo di Vicenza
☎ *0444 860561*

Villa Pojana, Miniscalchi Erizzo, Bettero, Chiarello

Via Castello, 21
Poiana Maggiore
☎ *0444 323014*

Via San Francesco, 2
Orgiano

Villa Fracanzan, Dal Ferro, Orgiano, Marsilio, Piovene Porto Godi

Contents

Printed in January 2009
by EBS Editoriale Bortolazzi-Stei
San Giovanni Lupatoto (Verona)
Italy